TWO DAYS IN
PANAMA

Stories of Sacred Awakening

ARMANDO MACHADO

Copyright © 2021 by Armando Machado

All rights reserved. No part of this publication in print or in electronic format may be reproduced, stored in a retrieval system, or transmitted in any form or by any means, electronic, mechanical, photocopying, recording, or otherwise without the prior written permission of the publisher.

The scanning, uploading, and distribution of this book without permission is a theft of the author's intellectual property. If you would like permission to use material from the book (other than for review purposes), please contact machado.cp0010@gmail.com. Thank you for your support of the author's rights.

Distribution by Bublish, Inc.

ISBN: 978-1-6470437-0-4 (Paperback)

Dedicated to my parents,
Ignacio y Ruby Machado

With gratitude to the Archdiocese of New York,
and to the pilgrims of World Youth Day Panama 2019
who shared with me their moments of sacred awakening.

CONTENTS

Hotel El Panamá 1

St. John Paul II Field (Saturday) 63

St. John Paul II Field (Sunday) 73

McDonald's restaurant on Vía España 77

Tocumen International Airport 93

Author's Notes 103

About the Author 105

HOTEL EL PANAMÁ

IN THE HOUR leading to the pope's closing Mass, multitudes of men, women and children walked toward the massive field to witness the historic event. And so, they were unofficial pilgrims of World Youth Day Panama 2019. The overnight vigil camping crowd was estimated at six hundred thousand. The closing Mass attendance estimate was seven hundred thousand. So evidently these unofficial but faithful pilgrims added one hundred thousand to the extraordinary but humble liturgical gathering.

They walked on various streets leading to the field. I saw them as I sat in the back seat of a taxi en route from my hotel to the morning Mass. They walked on the streets and on the sidewalks, amid traffic back-ups; many people were in vehicles also heading to the field. Words on the cab radio were those of two morning show announcers, a man and woman, speaking in Spanish, with joyful rapidness, about the same historic scene I was witnessing—the multitudes heading toward the pope's outdoor Mass.

The cab driver dropped me off, I think about three blocks away because of the traffic back-up. He said vehicles apparently were being diverted from the rear entrance area of the field. And he'd noted the front and main entrance area was cordoned off completely to vehicles; no regular civilian vehicles could get close. And that's why he took the route leading to the rear entrance, to get me closer to the field, for a shorter walk. I thanked him, paid him, exited the cab, and started walking fast like others heading the same way.

It was Sunday, January 27, at St. John Paul II Field (Metro Park) in Panama City. Mass started at 8:10 a.m., after the beloved pope greeted the cheering crowd as he rode around the field, standing in the fast-moving Popemobile (the vehicle from where he waves at crowds). I managed to take a decent photo with my cell phone as he was waving to the people from the vehicle. (And I got three good photos and a blurry picture of the pontiff the previous evening when he arrived at the same site for the vigil service, also on the Popemobile. And after the vigil, I took pictures of the original Our Lady of Fatima statue, as it was being carried from the altar and stage area).

It was a whirlwind weekend assignment for me—covering the last two days of this world-class retreat that was WYD Panama led in Spanish by the head of the Roman Catholic Church, Pope Francis, a son of Argentina. That alone made it an exceptionally significant journalistic task. But indeed, the entire weekend—leaving Newark Liberty International Airport late Friday night and arriving back at dawn on Monday—was exceptional for me as a journalist, a Catholic, and a son of Panama. (WYD Panama 2019 was held Jan. 22 to 27).

I was born in the city of Colón (We lived on Calle 6, across from a park, Parque 5 de Noviembre), about an hour drive from Panama City, the country's capital (and the WYD host city), and I was raised in New York, up in the Bronx, row house on Davidson Avenue (Fordham

Road area near Jerome Avenue; raised with an older brother and a younger sister). I have lived almost all my life in the United States—in the Northeast, the Northwest, and back to the Northeast. (The other languages spoken at WYD Panama were English, Italian, French, and Portuguese, mostly by several young-adult announcers, and by liturgical readers; and there were hymns sung in the various languages, including the theme song, "Here I Am, The Servant of the Lord").

My task was to write a news story for the Archdiocese of New York (Catholic New York, biweekly newspaper), on deadline that Monday in the Manhattan office, focusing on the WYD experience of members of the pilgrimage group from the archdiocese. I met up with them at 8:50 a.m. Saturday the 26th, before they started their 2.7-mile walking trek to the vigil and Mass site from Hotel El Panamá, where they were staying. I interviewed probably ten to twelve of them in the lobby—young-adult pilgrims as well as group coordinators. I interviewed people in English, Spanish, and Spanglish (mixing both languages within the same conversation and even the same sentence).

My primary goal was to first interview Josue, one of the young New York pilgrims. I had learned via a coordinator's text early Friday that Josue had been chosen to participate that evening in the Way of the Cross with the pope. Josue was in his twenties, also from the Bronx. I arrived at the lobby at 8:15 a.m. Saturday, and eagerly awaited there for the New York group to come down, but initially saw pilgrims from other states.

I finally saw one of the New York coordinators at 8:50 a.m., and I interviewed him— Brother Tyrone—then I met a woman who I thought was also a coordinator, but learned she was the mother of one of two priests in the group. So I interviewed her—there was still no Josue. Her name was Mercedes; she told me Josue would be down in a moment.

I believe in the meantime I interviewed a young pilgrim, also in his twenties. When I finally saw Josue for the first time, he was approaching one of several black leather sofas in the large lobby—in the waiting area 12 to 15 yards from the front counter. I was 99 percent sure it was him; he was all smiles—and evidently, he was almost certain who I was, seeing me with my pen and notebook in hand, and a photo ID card hanging from my neck (It was my Arch NY ID card. I had yet to go to the International Press Center to obtain my WYD press credentials.) Sra. Mercedes introduced us; Josue was still all smiles, apparently from the euphoria from having participated in the Way of the Cross the previous night with the pope. I asked both to sit on the sofa as I got my digital recorder ready, while making sure I did not drop pen, notebook, or recorder.

And, as I sat down on a low table in front of the sofa, I was certainly cherishing the moment; I was about to interview the main source of the story, a joyful young man who got to be in close proximity to the pope during a very special, faith-filled ceremony. And I knew that I would further interview Sra. Mercedes, as well as her son, Father Joseph. I interviewed her right there as I was interviewing Josue, as they sat on the sofa. I interviewed her priestly son later. The gleeful Josue told me about his unique experience, his pure delight in participating in the Way of the Cross with the pontiff. I took pictures of Josue, Sra. Mercedes, and others that I interviewed over a roughly 80-minute period before they began walking to the vigil site.

I then got a taxi and headed for the International Press Center (Atlapa Convention Center) to present my credentials permission letter and obtain my credentials and photo ID. I had yet to check into my hotel, the Hyatt Place, about three blocks from Hotel El Panamá on the opposite side of Vía España. I still had my carry-on with me when I was interviewing the Arch NY group members in the Hotel El Panamá lobby. I had tried checking in before walking to Hotel El Panamá, but I was told it was too early. After receiving my WYD press pass and a Panama flag from a friendly press center lady, I returned to the Hyatt Place by taxi before noon and was allowed to check in even though the official check-in time was later, 1:00 p.m. I believe.

I was exhausted from the overnight flight, I was hungry, and by then I believe I was feeling somewhat disoriented—a little overwhelmed with the fact that I was in the country of my birth, not having been there since 1991, and because of the reason I was there: to cover a world-class retreat led by the much beloved Pope Francis.

In my room at the Hyatt, I took off my shoes and took a nap, I believe starting on the sectional sofa and then on the bed. Later in the afternoon, it was back to the International Press Center to board one of the many buses that were shuttling journalists to and from the vigil and Mass site—still wearing the pants and polo shirt I started out with when I left Newark Airport the previous night, Friday (I traveled light, just the carry-on, with a change of clothes for Sunday morning).

I am a coffee drinker (one to two cups a day), but I didn't have coffee the entire weekend, and I hardly ate. I was assignment focused, and working on adrenaline. Besides, it was too hot to drink hot coffee, temperatures in the nineties plus humidity; and I don't like cold coffee drinks. And all told, I didn't need the caffeine; it was pure adrenaline. I probably lost two or three pounds during my two days in Panama *(dos días en Panamá)*. I remember the waistline of my pants feeling a little looser after returning to New York early Monday.

What follows are extended excerpts of the words of Arch NY pilgrims and coordinators I interviewed that fateful morning in the lobby of Hotel El Panamá. In subsequent pages are the words of pilgrims and coordinators from other countries – people I spoke with later Saturday at the vigil and Mass site, Sunday at a McDonald's on Vía España, and at Tocumen International Airport Sunday evening before boarding for my return flight. (Some interviews are translated from Spanish, followed in italics by the original words spoken in Spanish.)

I told half or more of the people I interviewed that I was Panama-born and New York-raised, and how extra important the assignment was for me because of my Panamanian roots; they all expressed delight and contentment. The Arch NY excerpts start with Josue, the chosen one.

Josue Rosario Cruz, 24, a parishioner of St. Anthony of Padua, the Bronx (and me, Armando Machado (AM):

AM: Josue, congratulations.
Josue: Thank you, man. I appreciate that.
AM: So, how did it go? *Acabo de conocer a la madre del padre* (I just met the mother of the father). [Mercedes, mother of Father Joseph.]
[Josue laughs.]
Josue: *Me adoptó* ("She adopted me"], he said smiling. [Sra. Mercedes is a family friend who sees Josue as if he were a grandson.]

AM: *Dime por favor, ¿cómo te fue anoche?* (Tell me please, how did it go for you last night?).

Josue: *Bueno, en el principio estaba como* (Well, at the start it was like) … Can I say it in English? [He laughs.]

AM: Oh, yeah, go ahead.

Josue: I was really excited. I was, like, feeling nervous. I was all over the place. But once the Holy Father came on stage, I just felt like a sense of peace came over me, you know. Honestly, it was like, it was amazing because I've been praying for that. I'm the type of guy who talks a lot, you know. I overthink things; and I've been praying for the Lord to calm my—to calm me down; calm the thoughts in my head, and so I can hear His voice more clearly. And honestly, after seeing the Holy Father up there at the *Vía Crucis* [Way of the Cross, in Santa María la Antigua Field], it felt as if that's what happened. I can now hear the voice of God a lot more clearly than I ever could before. I can give myself away a lot more, better, stronger, faster—without thinking it, without doubting it—just giving myself away completely, you know, without a problem.

AM: Because of this experience with the Way of the Cross?

Josue: "Yes." [Josue said with an exhausted sigh and smile.]

AM: And what did you do? What was your part?

Josue: My part was to carry the cross with the US delegation, and I got to stand in the back. Each country took a turn carrying the cross.

AM: So, you represented the Archdiocese of New York doing that?

Josue: USA.

AM: USA? The whole country?

Josue: The whole country.

AM: Wow. [So, it was Josue and several pilgrims from other US dioceses carrying the USA cross.]

[Josue laughed an affable, gregarious laugh that everyone in the Arch NY group came to know, and some already knew.]

Josue: And the greatest part about it was that the USA had the privilege, like Panama, to stand the closest to the pope up the stairs of the stage. We got to go up the stairs and stand there with Panama for a good five to ten seconds. Then they left and we started moving, but we were like, right there with the pope!

[Josue laughs, still elated.]

He was only like ten feet away. He gave the final blessing, and he gave like a homily type thing. From what I got out of it, I feel like we need to wake up to whatever is going on—not just, like, in the world but in the Catholic Church. Especially in the U.S., we need to wake up and start putting our foot down. Not being afraid in professing our faith. Not being afraid of doing what is right and doing what the Lord has called us to do. You know, I feel like we have not been firm in our faith. It started about 5:30 p.m. and it finished around 7:30 p.m. [The Way of the Cross]. He [the pope] waved at us. He talked about what it means to carry the cross, giving ourselves away to God. Trust in Mary, and then Mary takes us to the feet of Jesus. And not only that, to like, the youth to step up.

AM: Are you the one who told me recently that you went to the Charismatic Center [in the Bronx] a long time ago?

Josue: That was the call?

AM: Yeah. And that was a turning point for you? You're twenty-four now, right?

Josue: Yes.

AM: How old were you when that happened, when you were at the Charismatic Center? When you felt like there was a change in your life.

Josue: It was 2015 when everything happened.

AM: So, it was four years ago.

Josue: Yes. And I went to Ecuador on a mission trip not knowing anything about the faith. All I knew was, right, what happened in the Bible was real—that's all I knew.

AM: Oh, you went to Poland, right? [WYD 2016.]

Josue: I went to Poland.

AM: So, this is another turning point. Last night with the Way of the Cross, obviously, and this whole week?

Josue: Yeah.

AM: You could call it like a spiritual turning point.

Josue: Yes. Poland for me was a spiritual enlightenment. Not only that, but a confirmation of my faith. This one is more of a—it gave me the spiritual ammunition I need, and the strength that I need. Within all that, God took all the fear away from me—all the fear that I had in my heart, all the darkness that I had in my heart. He took it all out and gave me what I need to face whatever is going to be ahead of me from here on. If I give myself to God in the priesthood, or I give myself to God in marriage, or whatever it is, I know for sure God will always have my back.

AM: How many countries were represented?

Josue: It was fourteen stations—fourteen countries.

AM: How did you get chosen? What was the process?

Josue: From what I know—you could ask Mary Elise, she knows the whole thing—but from what I know, it was all God. He put it in someone's heart to ask Mary Elise that they needed someone, and God put it in Mary Elise's heart to ask Father J [Father Joseph Espaillat]. And Father J just said without thinking it, he said, Josue. And I was like, oh my gosh.

AM: So, you're going to go to breakfast now?

Josue: I'm going to go to breakfast—'cause I'm hungry.

AM: Before you go, *quédense ahí* (stay there). I want to take a picture of you. Can you put one of those sweaters on? [They were actually T-shirts).]

Josue: Oh yeah, I can do that. [Josue stands up to put on an Arch NY group T-shirt. Sra. Mercedes already had hers on.]

AM: For the picture.

Josue: *¿Sentado o parado?* (Sitting or standing?)

AM: *Ahí mismo, donde estaban sentando* (Right there, where you both were sitting). [And I take several pictures of Josue and Sra. Mercedes.]

[A few minutes later:]

Josue: This is my little sister.

AM: Oh, hi. My name is Armando.

Christie: Hi, I'm Christie [Apparently in her late teens.]

AM: Oh, good to meet you.

[Then I took some group photos.]

Sra. Mercedes Espaillat, mother of Father Joseph Espaillat II, pastor of St. Anthony of Padua, the Bronx, translated from Spanish:

AM: Sra. Mercedes, can you describe how you feel for him?

Sra. Mercedes: When I saw him last night, and he was with that smile of his, it was obvious that something had touched him. I told myself, that's my Josue. Then Christie, his sister, and I hugged each other, and we began to cry. But it was a cry of great joy, and I cannot explain it. At my age, he could be my grandson. And when I saw him, Christie became emotional. He is my spiritual grandson. We were close to the stage.

AM: Sra. Mercedes, ¿puede decir usted, cómo te sientes por él?

Sra. Mercedes: Cuando lo vi anoche, que él estaba con esa sonrisa, se veía que algo le había tocado. Yo me decía, ese es mi Josué. Es mi Josué. Entonces, Christie, la hermana, y yo nos abrazamos y empezamos a llorar. Pero era un lloro tan grande de alegría, que yo no puedo explicarlo. A mi edad, él puede ser mi nieto. Y cuando yo lo vi, Christie se emocionó. Él es mi nieto espiritual. Estábamos cerca del escenario.

Back to Josue:
AM: I'm from Colón, Panama. So I had to come. I'm here for the final two days. I couldn't make it for the whole week.

[Josue smiles and says it's good that I could be there for at least part of it.]

AM: Are you from the Dominican Republic or born in the US?

[He says yes, he was born in the US.]

Josue: I was born in Camp Pendleton [Marine Corps base, North San Diego County, California.] Both my parents were born in the Dominican Republic.

Sra. Mercedes again, translated from Spanish:
[She is from the Dominican Republic, immigrated with her family to New York when she was eight years old, and returned to the Dominican Republic after she got married.]

Sra. Mercedes: The police here have conducted themselves very well. They have treated us with much respect, and the event volunteers also; they say things like, 'what do you need? We are here to help.' Incredible…I was born in Santo Domingo.

AM: Okay. Thank you, Sra. Mercedes.

Sra. Mercedes: It has been a pleasure.

Sra. Mercedes: *La policía aquí se ha portado muy bien. Nos han tratado con mucho respeto. Y los voluntarios del evento también. Dicen: '¿Qué necesitan? Aquí estamos para ayudar. Increíble…Yo nací en Santo Domingo.*

AM: Gracias, Sra. Mercedes.

Sra. Mercedes: Ha sido un placer.

Brother Tyrone Davis, Executive Director, Office of Black Ministry, Arch NY:

(The first interview, before I met Sra. Mercedes and Josue, while waiting in the hotel lobby.)

Brother Tyrone: The young people were in great spirits, really enthusiastic about the whole experience, about meeting up with other young adults from around the world. I arrived Thursday. Our young people arrived Monday, and they were prepared to offer each other gifts.

Our young people prepared special wristbands to exchange. [Brother Tyrone gave me one of the wristbands. It reads: Office of Black Ministry—Archdiocese of New York; it is red, white, and blue, colors of the US and Panama flags.]

Junelle Addei, 20, a parishioner of Immaculate Conception Church, South Bronx:

(Her first World Youth Day)

Junelle: Honestly, I'm really loving it, simply because I think this is the most at peace that I've been, but also energetic—and so just to have those two emotions combined in one place. There are a bunch of people who probably feel the same way as I do. This makes me feel very grateful to have this experience.

I feel like I've been able to go further in my faith and my spirituality with God. I feel like I've been able to bond with my fellow scholars, and with other people that I've met here, and everybody else's energy from other countries. They have been so welcoming, so great—and just, I'm really enjoying it. And I've just—in a way I don't want it to end.

[Junelle said she was very grateful for receiving the Pierre Toussaint scholarship through Arch NY, which helped with most of the costs related to her WYD Panama trip.]

We learned about this about a year or two ago. And as soon as they asked us who would like to go, I said, I'm in, count me in there. I've had some time to rest up for tonight's prayer vigil. I've had some time to myself, for prayer and reflection and meditation.

Guadalupe Pimentel, 20, of Our Lady of Mount Carmel in the Bronx:

[She fell and hurt her knee the previous day when she also had a bad cough.]

Guadalupe: It still hurts, but I feel better [she says about her knee]. I feel very good about being here at World Youth Day. I feel like there is now something in me, something that has filled me. I feel a peace, a tranquility. And even though the days are long and heavy, I feel like I'm going along very well. And I know why I am here. I feel very good.

AM: Are you going to stay after the vigil overnight, until morning for the Mass?
GP: Yes, I have my backpack.
AM: Where are you from, your family?
GP: My family is from Mexico. I was born in New York…First, we were in the *pantalla* [event screen, earlier in the week], and there were rumors that he [the pope] was going to pass where we were. But I couldn't believe it. And then when we heard that it was true, we all ran to where the pope was, and there was a lady who wanted to see him. And I told her that she could stand in front of me.

The pope passed, and we all started to cry, we shouted. We took videos. And even though this was my second time seeing the pope. Yes, this was my second time seeing the pope passing, but this time I saw him closer [The first time was in WYD Poland 2016]. And just seeing him smile, and greeting everyone, it was a beautiful moment. And I wanted to share the video with my mom.

AM: So you took pictures and a video of that and you sent it to your mom. I imagine that she liked that very much.
GP: Yes, she liked it very much.

AM: I was born here in Panama.
GP: Oh, yes, that's true? I didn't know.

AM: I was born in Colón, Panama.

GP: Aha [she said with a smile].

AM: So it was important for me to be here, even though it's the last two days.

GP: Yes, that is good, especially for the Mass tomorrow morning. And I saw that you sent me an email message saying that you would be here. I just saw it; it is so good that you could make it here. Look at that—the coincidences [she said smiling].

Guadalupe Pimentel:

Guadalupe: Me siento muy bien estando aquí para la Jornada Mundial de la Juventud (JMJ). Me siento como si hay algo en mí como que se ha llenado. Siento una paz, una tranquilidad. Y aunque los días son muy largos y muy pesados, siento que voy muy bien, yo sé porqué estoy aquí. Me siento muy bien.

AM: ¿Te quedarás toda la noche en la vigilia para la misa en la mañana? Guadalupe: Sí, pero tengo la mochila [ella dijo con una sonrisa] ... Mi familia es de México; nací en Nueva York.

Primero estábamos en la pantalla, y había rumores que él [el papa] iba a pasar por donde estábamos, pero no lo podía creer. Y después cuando escuchamos que sí, todos corrimos a donde estaba pasando el papa y vi una señora que quería verlo. Entonces le digo: usted se puede poner delante de mí. Pasó el papa—y todos empezamos a llorar. Gritamos, agarramos video. Y aunque fue mi segunda vez; sí, es mi segunda vez que estoy viendo el papa así pasando; pero esta vez lo vi más cerca [primera vez era en JMJ

Polonia 2016] Y nada más viéndolo sonreír y que estaba saludando, era un momento muy bonito—y lo quise compartir con mi mamá el video.

AM: Así que tú cogiste fotos y video de eso y se lo mandaste a tu mamá. Me imagino que le gustó mucho eso ella.
Guadalupe: Sí, le gustó mucho.
AM: Yo nací aquí en Panamá.
Guadalupe: Ah ¿en verdad? Yo no sabía.
AM: Nací en Colón, Panamá.
Guadalupe: Ajá, *[dijo con una sonrisa].*

AM: Así que era importante para mí estar aquí—aunque sea que es los últimos dos días.
Guadalupe: Sí, qué bueno, especialmente para la misa mañana. Y me di cuenta que me mandó un correo electrónico, diciendo que iba a estar acá. Apenas ahorita lo miré, y ¡qué bueno que estás aquí! Sí, mira eso. Sí, las coincidencias *[ella dijo con una sonrisa].*

Adriana Sanes, 20, junior year at College of New Rochelle (NY), studying criminal justice and international studies:

(This is her first WYD)

Adriana: It's been an excellent experience; when I was blessed with the opportunity, I wasn't really sure what to expect. I'm here with the Office of Black Ministry. It's been life changing. I've really been humbled by this experience. It's been wonderful to be a part of it—like having the opportunity to be involved in all the activities, the catechesis.

And having the opportunity to see the pope—it's really been a beautiful experience. My experience here—one of the reasons why I decided to come was to strengthen my faith. And I think that has been done, you know? I realize that I'm not by myself in this. There are a lot of people my age who take their religion just as seriously.

And I think I'm going to be able to go back home with a lot more positive mindset, a lot more spirited attitude, that I can help bring back to my community.

Sra. Mercedes and Josue, in the lobby of Hotel El Panamá Saturday morning, after Machado interviewed them.

Members of the Arch NY World Youth Day group, in the Hotel El Panamá lobby area Saturday morning.

A larger group picture of the Arch NY group in the Hotel El Panamá lobby area Saturday morning.

One of a number of similar WYD welcoming signs at Tocumen International Airport; photo taken by Machado at dawn Saturday upon arriving in Panama.

Pope Francis arriving in the Popemobile to lead the Saturday Jan. 26 vigil service. The author took the four pictures two to three seconds apart.

Pope Francis arriving in the Popemobile to lead the Saturday Jan. 26 vigil service. The author took the four pictures two to three seconds apart.

Mary Elise, wearing flip-flops and with purse strap on left shoulder, directs her sub-group at Hotel El Panamá Saturday morning before they begin their walking trek to St. John Paul II Field for the vigil service.

Joyful WYD group from Nicaragua before the start of the Saturday vigil service at St. John Paul II Field.

AM Reflection:

It was during the closing Mass, after we all prayed the Our Father, and everyone gave their liturgical neighbors the sign of peace—many with handshakes and many with hugs—pilgrims, ministry leaders, journalists of the Church, and the multitudes that were unofficial pilgrims at the back of the great field, far from the pope and the altar.

This was a moment I will always remember as a turning point in my assignment, and indeed in my faith life—sharing the sign of peace during the largest Mass I have ever attended, celebrated by the pope in my birthland. Another special moment came a short while later during Communion—it was a spiritual uplift as I stood in one of many lines for the Eucharist, in fact it was a double line.

At first, I was in the double line in which a woman, probably in her late thirties, was the Eucharistic minister; she ran out of the Communion bread, left and came back with more; she later ran out of bread again but took a long time returning. A priest, probably in his mid-forties, eventually came and took over. I received the Eucharist from him.

After receiving the Bread of Life, I prayed, I believe a Hail Mary and a Glory Be, not sure. I probably had some jetlag; but those two prayers are what I often pray after Communion. I was assignment focused, but I felt obligated as a Church member to participate in the Mass. It was a significant, special assignment for me, and at times the two days felt surreal.

The sign of peace and the Eucharist that Sunday morning, and interviewing Josue the previous morning, about twenty-four hours earlier—these were the three most special moments for me during that weekend in January 2019. January was also the month of my birth, fifty-nine years earlier. At World Youth Day 2019 it evidently was the month of my rebirth – rebirth of spirit in my homeland, my birth land, Panama. I was born in Colón, on the Atlantic and Caribbean side. I guess I was reborn in Panama City, on the Pacific side.

Just like Adriana, I also felt blessed. I felt blessed as a journalist covering World Youth Day, as a Catholic because I was among many fellow Catholic Latino journalists and multicultural Catholic faithful, and as a son of Panama, because this very special gathering led by the pope was occurring in my motherland.

And in my thoughts tonight (Saturday Aug. 31, 2019):

I wonder how I managed to keep going, evidently working on adrenaline, having no coffee at all that weekend in Panama City. I think about the Colombian nun I met Sunday evening inside the McDonald's on Vía España; she came a little after I got there, doing the same thing I was—watching the TV news, the live coverage of the pope's ceremonial departure from Tocumen airport. I left my table and walked to hers and asked her if I could interview her about World Youth Day. She said yes, and we began to talk.

Most, if not all, of the weekend felt somewhat surreal to me; at times I felt a little disoriented or dizzy. But I knew it was very real, I was cherishing every hour, every single minute. It apparently was a spiritual transformation, and I didn't realize it at the time.

Rose Clottey, 30, of St. Luke's parish in the Bronx:

Rose: We are part of the Ghanaian community of St. Luke's. This is my third World Youth Day. I went to Madrid [2011] and then I went to Poland [2016]. I didn't get to go to Brazil [2013].

AM: So you've seen the pope before?

Rose: Yeah, a couple of times. This week has been amazing. It's been a pilgrimage. It's been rewarding, basically. The catechesis lessons have been great. The Masses have been great. On Tuesday, we got to meet with all the pilgrims from America, in one of the conference centers. The bishop from Los Angeles—he gave a really great talk. And so it's very rewarding. I think I had my turning point a while ago when I started [WYD Madrid 2011]. But it's just great to reaffirm it every single time.

Stephanie Boadu, 27, also from St. Luke's parish:

Stephanie: This is my second. I was in Poland [2016]. Panama has been great. The locals have been very welcoming. They cheer you on. They make you really proud to be Catholic. And like Rose said, the catechesis has been good. I like the theme for this year: I Am a Servant of the Lord. The books have talked about our fiat, saying yes to God's calling; so that was very powerful. But yeah, just being around everybody here, all the young Catholics, has been a good experience.

AM: So you grew up Catholic also?

Stephanie: Yes, I was born Catholic, been a Catholic—going to stay Catholic [she laughs, looking at Rose, who smiles]. My faith is a huge part of my whole life, and for my family as well. It guided me throughout college; especially during tough times, I turned to my faith. It's what leads me. It's what keeps me going.

AM: Thank you much. I appreciate it.
Rose: It was nice meeting you.
Stephanie: Thank you so much.
AM: Maybe I'll see you tomorrow at the Mass.
Rose: Yes.

Early in the interview, I told Rose and Stephanie that I went to St. Luke's grade school (first to fifth grade), that I received my First Holy Communion in the parish church, their parish. They were both genuinely and pleasantly surprised, evidently wanting to know more. But I quickly turned the conversation back to the interview, mindful that the group was preparing backpacks to leave for the vigil site, St. John Paul II Field (Metro Park).

Juliemarie Hernandez, 20, parishioner of St. Anthony of Padua, in the Bronx:

Juliemarie: Yeah, I did [see Josue last night at the Way of the Cross]. I was very proud to see that we were represented—being one of the groups, of the many American groups, to be chosen, to be represented in the Way of the Cross. Participating in this World Youth Day means for me—it's a new beginning. Like a sacrament, a new beginning to a new way of life. When I get back to my parish to change things up as a youth minister myself, there's definite change that can happen, and things that we can do differently, that we've observed from being in this community in Panama.

We saw him [Pope Francis] earlier in the week—he passed by us when he was coming from the main stage. So we've seen him twice. It was really cool because we got to see him up close. It was very exciting; he was probably about ten feet away. It was like you see someone on the TV screen so much, and someone with so big a role, and you get to see him up close, it's a different feeling. Going to an event and you learn something new, and you're bringing that aspect back home, I feel like little by little we'll make a change. [She's vice president of *Jóvenes Con Poder, JCP* (Young People With Power), a youth group at her parish].

Moises Cepeda, 18, from St. Gabriel's Church, New Rochelle, NY:

Moises: It's a way to travel all over the world while staying in one place (right here in Panama). I've met people from all over the world—and I think that's something that's really nice. So this is a way to see different cultures and meet different people. It's been a great experience. Yeah, I saw the pope for a couple of seconds. [Moises was at the Way of the Cross, but was far from the stage and watched one of the large screens]. It was nice to see all the different countries coming together, and having the same ideal, doing something for the same cause.

AM: OK, Moises; thank you much. I appreciate it.
Moises: *Mucho gusto* (My pleasure).

Father Benjamin Palacios, pastor of St. Gabriel Church, New Rochelle, NY, translated from Spanish:

AM: It was important for me to be here because I was born here in Panama, in Colón, Panama.
Fr. Benjamin: Wow…I lived in Panama for a year.

AM: Oh, yes?

Fr. Benjamin: And what are you gathering? [What kind information was I seeking].

AM: I'm here gathering comments from the group from New York, before they head to the vigil. I spoke with a young woman from your church, Juliemarie Hernandez?

Fr. Benjamin: Juliemarie? No…

AM: Oh, she's from another church. Yes, she was from another church. Oh, here, I spoke with Moises Cepeda.

[The pastor says yes, Moises is from his parish. I ask him how he would describe the importance of World Youth Day].

Fr. Benjamin: Here the youths strengthen their faith. Here the youths make a commitment. They make a commitment to help build a new Church. It is super important. In World Youth Day the young people grow strong in the faith, they find their vocation—and they commit themselves to becoming evangelists, evangelizing other young people. The Way of the Cross was a great message.

Padre Benjamín Palacios:

AM: Era importante para mí estar aquí porque yo nací aquí en Panamá, en Colón, Panamá.

Padre Benjamín: Wow…Yo viví en Panamá un año.

AM: ¿Oh, sí?

Padre Benjamín: ¿Y que estás tomando?

AM: Estoy tomando comentarios del grupo de Nueva York, antes que se vayan a la vigilia. Hablé con una joven de su iglesia, ¿Juliemarie Hernández?

Padre Benjamín: ¿Juliemarie? No…

AM: *Oh, she's from another church. Yes, she must be from another church. Oh, aquí, hablé con Moisés Cepeda. [El pastor dijo que sí, Moisés es de su parroquia.]*
Padre Benjamín: *Aquí la juventud se fortalece en la fe. Aquí la juventud se compromete. Ellos se comprometen a ayudar a construir una nueva Iglesia.*
Es súper importante. En el World Youth Day los jóvenes aumentan su fe, encuentran su vocación—y ellos se comprometen a ser evangelizadores de otros jóvenes… Fue un mensaje muy grande, el Vía Crucis.

Cynthia Psencik, Director, Arch NY Youth Ministry Office (also at El Hotel Panamá, Saturday morning):

AM: Oh, hola Cynthia. Good to see you.
Cynthia: Good to see you too.
[Most from the group around us are still getting ready to head out.]

AM: Can we step away just for a few minutes before you leave?
Cynthia: Okay, yes.
AM: How did it go last night with the Way of the Cross?

Cynthia: It was beautiful. I think, obviously one of the most touching moments, for me personally, was that they highlighted Nuestra Señora de la Altagracia, patroness of the Dominican Republic where my family is from. I was born in New York City, but my parents are from the Dominican Republic. Just to see the Dominican Republic highlighted on screen with our *vestimentas* [traditional clothing], with our cultural customs, dress, especially because in our country the abuse of women is so prevalent; and the fact that that was the intention that was read—the protection, the dignity, holding the dignity of women. I think it was just very touching to see Our Lady of Altagracia. And of course, to see one of our young people there with the Holy Father was very touching.

AM: Josue?

Cynthia: Yes, Josue.

AM: Alright, so what's the plan for today?

Cynthia: Well, the plan for today, we're now getting ready to go to the site where the vigil with the Holy Father is going to happen tonight. And tomorrow will be the closing Mass with the Holy Father, where also the next World Youth Day will be announced. So we're getting ready. We're getting our legs ready… It will be a long walk. This is World Youth Day, the pilgrimage that we make toward the vigil site is the actual term that we use for World Youth Day, so on our way there we'll be praying, we'll be singing, we'll be meeting other pilgrims—all walking to hear what the Holy Father has to say for us tonight… Everybody will most likely stay there [overnight]. Everybody has sleeping bags. We camp out all night, and so we're there in the morning when the Holy Father has Mass.

Mary Elise Zellmer, Assistant Director, Arch NY Young Adult Outreach:

Mary Elise: The USCCB (US Conference of Catholic Bishops) reached out to me and they asked me to recommend a person.

AM: And why did you recommend Josue?

Mary Elise: I just think he's so vibrant and full of life, and I thought that he would do a great job representing us. He's a true New Yorker, and he just seemed to have it all.

AM Oh, I see. So how is it going so far?

Mary Elise: It's going amazing. Everybody's just been so enthusiastic, and really enjoying themselves, getting fully into the whole, uhm, getting fully, a like, sorry... [Mary Elise lost her train of thought at that moment, evidently a little tired, maybe exhausted, from all the administrative decisions she was making that week for World Youth Day activities that she had to oversee, while also maintaining her role as sort of a mentor for the young adult pilgrims]... You know it's amazing because we got to see Pope Francis as well.

AM: Yeah, I was going to ask you about that. Was that your first time you've seen the pope?

Mary Elise: That was not my first time, but for most of the young people that was their first time seeing the pope.

AM: Oh, you've been to other World Youth Days?

Mary Elise: I've been to other World Youth Days. And I've gone to the Vatican, and stuff like that [she laughs a joyful laugh]. Like Catholic veterans.

AM: What kind of reaction did you get from the young people who it was the first time for them [I could have phrased the question more eloquently. I was tired from the overnight flight. I was hungry and sleepy. And Mary Elise and the group seemed just about ready to begin their walking trek to the vigil site. I was asking questions quickly; she was replying quickly].

Mary Elise: They were absolutely touched and emotional—very excited. One of the girls, she even climbed a pole in order to be able to see him. And not being sure which side of the street he was going to be on, so everybody would run back and forth to the different streets. So people were really, really hoping to see him; and the fact that we did was absolutely amazing… It's a total number of fifty-three pilgrims from the Archdiocese of New York (forty-four young adult pilgrims and nine coordinators).

AM: So how do you feel about the whole thing? You're one of the lead organizers.

Mary Elise: It was—it was really good [she said, a bit distracted]. Armando, can I come back in a minute?

AM: Okay.

Mary Elise walked away hurriedly. She evidently realized she needed to get to something very important before the group started heading out of the lobby of Hotel El Panamá. She saw group members picking up their camping gear, apparently moments away from exiting the building.

A short while later, I saw her sub-group taking pictures with her just outside the lobby, in a ceilinged but open area—then they formed a circle and she led them in prayer. And then they began their walking journey to join the other Arch NY sub-groups on the way to the vigil. And so apparently, she cut short the interview because she wanted to make sure partly—probably mainly—that she led her assigned group in prayer before the trek began. I believe there were three sub-groups, hers had fifteen to eighteen pilgrims, ready for a vigil and Mass, the last two days of World Youth Day Panama 2019.

I did not communicate with Mary Elise again until the next day, Sunday Jan. 27, in the afternoon via email, hours after the closing Mass. I never found their field section on Saturday or Sunday amid the multitudes in the multiple lettered and numbered field sections. I was in my hotel room at the Hyatt Place, a few blocks from Hotel El Panamá in downtown Panama City.

Using my cell phone, I emailed Mary Elise asking for her final assessment, her reaction to the WYD week. She emailed me back later in the afternoon, and in her email, she cc'd Cynthia, asking her to do the same if she'd like to, and Cynthia did—both women writing from their hearts, with words of joy and hope:

Mary Elise emailed: These are some really special young people. I know they won't leave what they encountered and learned behind in Panama but will bring it with them [back to New York.]

Cynthia emailed: Being a part of this week helped me to witness the beauty of God's Church. We were all here because we love our faith.

AM Reflection:

Theirs were the second and third main set of interview comments in the first story I wrote. Josue's was the main set of comments—he was the key source, the main interview, the young man chosen by the office of the US Bishops to participate in the Way of the Cross with Pope Francis. In a follow-up story I wrote about WYD Panama—that story was based on additional interviews I had with pilgrims and coordinators in the Arch NY group, comments that did not make it into the first story—as well as interviews I had of pilgrims and coordinators from other countries—from Panama, from Colombia, from France, from Belgium, and from other nations. The commonality, of course, from the people I interviewed from Arch NY and from people of other countries, was the pure joy, the absolute joy; there was hope and faith and sincerity that came from the words of every single person I interviewed throughout that special weekend.

Both times that I witnessed Pope Francis speak, at the vigil service and the next morning at the closing Mass, I also witnessed every single person around me paying close, faith-filled attention. And there was the McDonald's on Vía España, where I interviewed the nun from Colombia early Sunday evening. The McDonald's is pretty much halfway between the two hotels, closer to Hotel El Panamá.

And there were interviews I had at the Tocumen International Airport Sunday night while waiting more than two hours for my return flight—pilgrims and coordinators from France, Belgium, the Congo, and South Korea. But that was the commonality—the pure joy and sincerity, hope and faith in all the words spoken in the different interviews. It was obviously a special turning point in the lives of many people, especially those experiencing their first World Youth Day. It was a turning point in their spiritual life; it was a sacred awakening.

Father Joseph Espaillat, pastor of St. Anthony of Padua Church, the Bronx, son of Sra. Mercedes:

Father Espaillat: It means a lot. Their spiritual growth from a pilgrimage is very powerful. This pilgrimage in specific is very, very meaningful… There are a lot of fruits, I believe, that will be coming from this—not only vocations but also just people committed to Christ and to the

Church through the intercession of Our Lady, walking in the footsteps of Our Lady.

It's meaningful for a lot of them because a pilgrimage is sacrifice, and many of them have gone through a lot in life. And it shows them that in walking through a pilgrimage, it's like walking through life. There's going to be ups, there's going to be great moments, and there's going to be a lot of downs. For this group in particular, I know that it's going to be very, very fruitful and very beneficial.

AM: Okay. *Muchas gracias, padre* [Thank you much, father].
Father Joseph: Alright, thank you.

Diane Botta, 30, from Basilica of Regina Pacis, in Brooklyn (Diocese of Brooklyn):

(She traveled with the Arch NY group through friendships with pilgrims in that group.)

Diane: Quite honestly, I felt like, A, it's kind of like a once in a lifetime experience. B, I guess you could say I had an experience that really, really strengthened my faith a couple of years ago. And it's hard to find other young Catholics to share that community with sometimes. Being in an environment with so many different people who share the same values can be very strengthening, I think, in a day and age when it's not very popular to be religious.

AM: So how would you describe the whole experience so far?
Diane: It's been hot; it's been crowded [she says with a laugh]. But it's been very moving. I think the Way of the Cross last night was very

touching. I really liked the dance performances that they had, just how detailed all the reflections were for every station. I thought that was really nice.

AM: So, you're friends with people from the Archdiocese of New York. That's why you're with them?

Diane: Yeah, I've done two [other] pilgrimages with the archdiocese. We did a pilgrimage to Fatima; we did a pilgrimage to Lourdes.

Daniel Genn, Associate Director, Arch NY Youth Ministry Office:

Daniel: I work with the archdiocese for the Office of Youth Ministry. I work with Cynthia, yeah. It's been great. It's been busy—and long and tiring and hot. But it's been great. The morning catechesis [yesterday] was really beautiful, the reflection that the bishop from Miami gave on hope—it was really beautiful, and there were opportunities for all to go to confession.

Stephanie Vargas, 32, from Precious Blood parish, Milford, Connecticut:

(She was one of several people from outside the New York archdiocese who joined with Arch NY.)

Stephanie: It's just been an amazing experience, seeing the joy of other young adults. You go on the subway and you hear people chanting, saying: You're the youth of the pope. It's really inspiring just having that. It was beautiful [Way of the Cross]. I thought it was really profound. We were in Section B-2, so a little farther than we were for the opening ceremony. We were watching the screens. One of the guys from St. Anthony's actually helped carry the cross for the country.

AM: Oh yeah, Josue.

Stephanie: Yeah, Josue. And I thought that was really nice, how they had different stations being represented by different countries.

AM: So, what is your hope for you personally in your spiritual growth?

Stephanie: My hope is to find how I can live more according to God's will day to day and be more joyful and be a light to the world that seems to be eschewing religion.

Yet for us it's everything, right? Jesus is everything, and everyone [in secular society] seems to be like pushing that away. And now seeing all these young adults, these young people just on fire for their faith—it is inspiring to show that you can change the world.

AM: Okay, Stephanie, thank you much. I appreciate it.

Stephanie: Thank you.

AM: What is your name? [I ask Stephanie to confirm her full name. As she tells me, I see Leah passing by.]

AM: Oh. Hi, Leah.

Leah: How are you? Good to see you.

AM: Good to see you.

[Leah Dixon works with Brother Tyrone; she is Associate Director, Arch NY Black Ministry Office.]

End of Saturday Jan. 26 morning interviews inside the Hotel El Panamá lobby.

Original Statue of Our Lady of Fatima, as it was being carried off after the Saturday vigil service.

Machado after the Saturday vigil service, as many pilgrims walked about taking pictures and taking in the extraordinary moment while soft event music continued.

Faithful, unofficial pilgrims walking toward St. John Paul II Field for the Sunday morning closing Mass. Photo taken by Machado from the back seat of the taxi he was in on the way to the Mass.

A street vendor organizes his WYD Panama merchandise while unofficial pilgrims make their way to the closing Mass.

Eager, unofficial pilgrims as they entered the rear area of St. John Paul II Field (Metro Park) for the Sunday morning closing Mass.

Many unofficial pilgrims upon entering the rear entrance of St. John Paul II Field for the Sunday morning closing Mass.

Machado captured this joyful moment as Pope Francis was chauffeured around the perimeter of St. John Paul II Field Sunday morning when the pope arrived to celebrate the WYD closing Mass.

The author inside the makeshift Media Center (large tent) at St. John Paul II Field, Sunday morning after the closing Mass.

Sister Luisa Teresa inside the McDonald's restaurant after being interviewed by Machado Sunday evening.

ST. JOHN PAUL II FIELD (SATURDAY)

SATURDAY JAN. 26, LATE AFTERNOON, ST. JOHN PAUL II FIELD:

Marian Arroyo, 25, home parish is Iglesia Inmaculada Concepción Pozos Santa Ana, San José, Costa Rica, translated from Spanish:

MARIAN: THIS IS my first World Youth Day, yes. The Way of the Cross was very emotional, because at every station there was a special prayer intention. *(Es mi primer World Youth Day. Si, el Vía Crucis, fui. Fue muy emotivo porque en cada estación del Vía Crucis se rezó por una intención especial).* And it was, well, the unity of all the young people praying for themes such as the ecology, and care for the world, the planet, and continuing to struggle for peace in each of our countries. We will be here in this vigil site overnight until tomorrow morning, for the Mass. From our parish we have seventeen people, most of them youths.

We belong to a religious order called Los Agustinos Recoletos. It is all over the world, and in Costa Rica they have a mission site. *(Pertenecemos a una orden de religiosos que se llama Los Agustinos Recoletos. Están por todo el mundo, y también en Costa Rica tienen su misión.)* [She says that in her immediate family she was the only child.]

I think that in my extended family, I am the first one to come to one of these events. I hope that in future generations in my family, or cousins, nephews, or children of cousins, that they will also attend World Youth Day. I feel privileged to be here, and to be part of a Church movement that helps build a better world, and to be part of that dream that the pope has. I saw him pass by in the car [the Popemobile].

LATER, SATURDAY EVENING:

María Leticia Sánchez, 22, of Panama, WYD volunteer, translated from Spanish:

[The choir music was loud; we both shouted a bit during the interview, so that we could hear each other.]

AM: Did you participate in most of the events this week?

María Leticia: No, because I was serving as a volunteer, so I could not participate in all the events this week. I just saw when he [the pope] arrived around the city. Now this is the second time [the vigil service]. I feel very privileged and blessed by having Pope Francis here—and for the second time having a pope here in Panama [Pope John Paul II visited Panama in 1983]. And I became a volunteer thanks to an agency in charge of scholarship programs for Panamanian students, for a scholarship to study Italian and serve as an interpreter here during World Youth Day. I prepared for eight months, and I traveled to Italy and learned the language to serve World Youth Day pilgrims, from Italy and from all over the world.

AM: So, you speak Italian well?

María Leticia: Yes, yes, I learned sufficiently. Well, I've had ambitions for visual media, and also for print journalism. Well, first I'm aspiring to finish my studies and later enter TV journalism, Panamanian and international.
AM: So, you want to be a TV reporter?
María Leticia: Or more. I am studying production. Well, whichever comes out good first, that's where I will be climbing.
AM: And how old are you?
María Leticia: Twenty-two.
AM: And what church do you go to; what is your parish?
María Leticia: It is in the city of La Chorrera; it is San Francisco de Paula Church, and Immaculate Conception Church.

As I began to ask María Leticia about her Catholic upbringing, she said "Yes" quickly, that she was grateful to her parents for the faith-filled way they raised her. We both started whispering at that point; the music had just ended, and she gestured that the interview had to end because the first vigil speaker was about to start addressing the multitudes. We both smiled and laughed quietly. She was still sitting on the ground, her back resting on a fence, and several other young volunteers were sitting the same way to her right. And I was still on my right knee just to her left, with notebook resting on my upper left leg. I said to her, "Okay, gracias." She smiled again and said "Gracias," turning her head toward the stage.

I stood up and took several steps away; she remained sitting on the ground alongside the other volunteers; she was at the end of a row of volunteers sitting on the ground, so she was by a wide isle that separated two sections for the crowd, not far from the very front seating area, maybe twenty-five yards from that area, and forty yards from the stage where the vigil activities were taking place—coordinators speaking words of inspiration, and choir members singing gentle hymns with instrumental accompaniment. (It was 7:23 p.m. when the interview ended after 3 minutes and 40 seconds. It was between day and night, closer to night.)

María Leticia Sánchez [*La música era ruidosa, así que estábamos gritando un poco durante la entrevista, para poder escucharnos.*]

AM: *¿Participaste en la mayoría de los eventos esta semana?*

María Leticia: No, porque estuve trabajando como voluntaria, así que no podía participar en todo los eventos esta semana. Solamente lo vi cuando llegó y fue por la ciudad. Ahora es la segunda vez [la vigilia]. Me siento bastante privilegiada y bendecida por tener al papa Francisco, y por segunda vez en Panamá a un papa [El papa Juan Pablo II visitó Panamá en 1983]. Y quedé como voluntaria gracias a un convenio a cargo de la ejecución de beca a estudiantes panameños de escasos recursos, una beca para estudiar italiano y ser intérprete en la Jornada Mundial de la Juventud. Me preparé por ocho meses, viajé también a Italia y aprendí el idioma para servir en la Jornada a los peregrinos, de Italia y también de todo el mundo.

AM: *¿Así que hablas Italiano bien?*

María Leticia: Sí, sí. Lo aprendí lo suficiente. Bueno, he tenido ambición de periodismo visual, y también el área de periódico, así que yo primero aspiro a terminar mi estudios que me falta un año y luego entrar en periodismo de televisión panameña como la internacional.

AM: ¿Como reportera en la televisión?
María Leticia: O más que eso. Estoy estudiando producción, pero pues lo que me salga primero allí iré escalando.

AM: ¿Y cuántos años tienes?
María Leticia: Veintidós.

AM: ¿Cuál es su iglesia, su iglesia principal?
María Leticia: En la ciudad La Chorrera, allí está la Iglesia de San Francisco de Paula, y también la Inmaculada Concepción.

∽∘∾

Empecé a preguntarle a María Leticia sobre su fe católica, como ella creció católica. Y me dijo que sí, que ella está muy agradecida por la manera que su mamá y papá la criaron, con mucha fe. La música termina; empezamos a susurrar en ese momento.

María Leticia: Sí, exactamente, sí [ella dijo con rapidez].

Ella indicó que la entrevista se tenía que terminar porque los coordinadores en el escenario iban a empezar a hablar. Los dos nos sonreímos, riendo bajito. Y le dije "Okay, gracias". Ella se quedó sentada en el suelo, y yo me levanté de mi rodilla derecha).

THE VIGIL SERVICE BEGINS:

During the vigil message, Pope Francis said:

We have watched that beautiful presentation about the Tree of Life [dance performance]. It shows us how the life that Jesus gives us is a love story, a life history that wants to blend with ours and sink roots in the soil of our own lives. That life is not a salvation up 'in the cloud' and waiting to be downloaded, a new 'app' to be discovered, or a technique of mental self-improvement.

Still less is it a 'tutorial' for finding out the latest news. The salvation the Lord offers us is an invitation to be part of a story interwoven with our personal stories. It is alive and wants to be born in our midst so that we can bear fruit just as we are, wherever we are and with everyone all around us.

The Lord comes there to sow and to be sown. He is the first to say 'yes' to our lives and history, and he wants us to say 'yes' along with him.

Later in the vigil message, the pope said:

In a few moments, we will encounter the living Jesus in Eucharistic adoration. You can be sure that he has many things to say to you, about different situations in your lives, families, and countries.

Face-to-face with him, don't be afraid to open your heart to him and ask him to renew the fire of his love, so that you can embrace life with all its frailty and flaws, but also with its grandeur and beauty. May he help you to discover the beauty of being alive.

Do not be afraid to tell him that you too want to be part of his love story in this world, that you are ready for something greater.

Friends, when you meet Jesus face-to-face, I ask you also to pray for me, so that I too will be unafraid to embrace life, to care for its roots and say, like Mary, 'Let it be done, according to Your word.'

After the pope's vigil message, the announcers told the pilgrims that the Adoration of the Blessed Sacrament would begin; and so it did, with prayer, choir music, and contemplative silence.

At the end of the vigil, the original statue of Our Lady of Fatima, which was on display on the altar and stage area, was carried in procession and placed upon the back of an open truck, with accompanying music. The truck was driven slowly away on the perimeter of the large field. Many of the faithful walked beside the truck, taking pictures of the statue. (The statue arrived in Panama Jan. 21 and was transported back to Portugal Jan. 29).

AM talking into recorder (audio notes to myself):

Repeating what a male event singer is singing at the end of the evening vigil, as I walked and wandered about like many others: *"Estos días han sido muy inolvidables; estos días han sido muy increíbles"*. Remember that: These days have been unforgettable; these days have been incredible. In a few days all of us will be back to our cities, our countries—we will never forget these days. That's a paraphrase—we will never forget these days—everything else is a direct quote. This is a male lead singer of one of the vigil music groups. It's about a quarter to nine, a now darkened

Saturday evening, the 26th of January, World Youth Day, Panama 2019, at Campo San Juan Pablo II (St. John Paul II Field), Panama City.

Pamela Quesada, 23, of Iglesia Dulce Nombre de Jesús (Arquidiócesis de San José, Costa Rica), translated from Spanish:

[Near the stage toward the end of the vigil service, while many people walked around taking pictures and taking in the surreal, euphoric moment under the night sky.]

AM: You were here all this week since Tuesday?

Pamela: Yes, all week since Tuesday. It has been super impressive; it fills one very much. It has been a week of great experience, of many emotions of encountering Christ—who really fills you. We all have a mission of listening to the pope, being able to listen to his words that help us grow day by day in the faith. I went last night to see the Way of the Cross. There were different countries represented in carrying the cross.

I am a Catholic since I was born. The Catholic Church for us has been super important. It has filled us with values, in believing in Christ. It is the Church that Jesus formed, that he founded…within her…

[A male coordinator on stage began talking. I could not decipher some of Pamela's words. I interviewed her in the darkened evening, but in a well-lit area near the stage, at the end of vigil service, with musicians still performing, and many people just walking about and taking photos].

[During my interview with Pamela, a woman at a mic on stage was speaking words of faith and joy, as well as do's and don'ts instructions for the rest of the overnight gathering.]

Pamela Quesada:
AM: *¿Tú estabas aquí toda la semana, desde el martes?*

Pamela: Si, toda la semana, si, desde el martes. Pues ha sido súper impresionante—llena a uno bastante. Ha sido una semana de experiencia, de emociones, de encuentro con Cristo, que realmente llena a uno. Todos venimos con una misión de escuchar al papa, escuchar su palabras que nos hagan crecer día con día en la fe. Sí, fui anoche a ver el Vía Crucis. Exacto, diferentes países tomando la cruz.

Soy Católica de nacimiento. La Iglesia católica para nosotros ha sido súper importante. Nos ha llenado de valores, a creer en Cristo. Es la iglesia que realmente Jesús formó, fundó.

ST. JOHN PAUL II FIELD (SUNDAY)

THE NEXT MORNING, SUNDAY JAN. 27, ST. JOHN PAUL II FIELD (METRO PARK) CLOSING MASS:

IN WELCOMING REMARKS, Archbishop José Domingo Ulloa of Panama thanked the pope for allowing WYD Panama to be planned and celebrated with a Marian theme and with "a style very much Latin American and Caribbean *(un estilo muy latinoamericano y caribeño)."*

In the homily, Pope Francis said:

In Jesus, the promised future begins and becomes life. When? Now. Yet not everyone who was listening felt invited or called. Not all the residents of Nazareth were prepared to believe in someone they knew and had seen grow up, and who was now inviting them to realize a long-awaited dream. Not only that, but they said: Is not this Joseph's son?

The same thing can also happen with us. We do not always believe that God can be that concrete and commonplace, that close and real, and much less that he can become so present and work through somebody like a neighbor, a friend, a relative.

You, dear young people, are not the future but the now of God. He invites you and calls you in your communities and cities to go out and find your grandparents, your elders, to stand up and with them to speak out and realize the dream that the Lord has dreamed.

Pope Francis, in his closing remarks, told the young people:

(After giving thanks to government leaders from Panama and other countries in attendance, and to all who made World Youth Day Panama 2019 possible.)

And to you, dear young people, a big 'thank you.' Your faith and joy have made Panama, America and the entire world shake! As we have heard so many times in these days in the song of this World Youth Day: 'As your pilgrim people we are gathered here today from every continent and city.' We are on a journey, keep walking, keep living the faith and sharing it. Do not forget that you are not the tomorrow, you are not the 'meantime.' You are the now of God.

I ask you not to let the fervor of these days grow cold. Go back to your parishes and communities, to your families and your friends, and share this experience, so that others can resonate with the strength and enthusiasm that is yours. With Mary, keep saying 'yes' to the dream that God has sown in you.

And please, do not forget to pray for me. Thank you. (*Y por favor, no se olviden de rezar por mí. Gracias*).

And then Cardinal Kevin Farrell, noted:

(Head of the Vatican's Dicastery for Laity, the Family and Life)
As the Holy Father has said, we must now leave here and put into practice everything that we have learned.

And the next World Youth Day will be in Portugal *(será en Portugal)*. [Wide applause]. And some repeat 'Portugal!' several times, and some again repeat: That is the youth of the pope! *(¡Esa es la juventud del papa!)*.

End of Closing Mass, Sunday morning Jan. 27.

MCDONALD'S RESTAURANT ON VÍA ESPAÑA

SUNDAY EVENING, INSIDE MCDONALD'S ON VÍA ESPAÑA:

I APPROACHED A nun as she was looking up at a TV monitor mounted on the wall, watching live coverage of the farewell ceremony for the pope at Tocumen Airport—which is what I was watching too for thirty minutes or more before she arrived and sat a couple of tables from where I was sitting. And the TV coverage continued as we spoke.

Sister Luisa Teresa García, 64, from the Franciscana Misioneras de Maria Auxiliadora (order of nuns in Colombia), translated from Spanish:

Sister Luisa Teresa: I am Colombian, but I am on mission in Cuba. I came with the group from Cuba. I attended almost all the events, with all the participants.

AM: Did you go to the Mass this morning?

Sister Luisa Teresa: I didn't go to it. I tried. But we arrived too late, because there were so many people. There were too many people to be able to get through [from the rear of the field]. But in any case, all the events we attended were wonderful, and the experience was incredible. The group of youths from Cuba were with us, and members of our [religious] community. It was for us a great joy to be able to come here, and for them [the youths from Cuba] to experience the greatness of our faith and of our Church, sharing this together with youths from all over the world, so that they don't feel alone; that they instead experience the Church with others from throughout the world.

AM: Yes, you're right.

Sister Luisa Teresa: And well, the words of the pope, the voice of the pope, it encourages all of us *(nos alienta a todos)*, the youth, the adults, to live our faith with joy and with enthusiasm—and as the pope says, without being afraid. To live with joy and with enthusiasm. And especially to the youths he said they should not lose the burning passion in their hearts *(el ardor en su corazón)*, that it was worth all the efforts, all the struggles, everything they had to do to get here, in order to obtain this experience, in order to get to know so many other people. And above all, to get to know Jesus more—and to be His witnesses in the world, in the place where each of them finds himself or herself.

AM: So which events did you attend this week?

Sister Luisa Teresa: I was at the welcoming Mass [at Santa María la Antigua Field]. And I was at the dinner for the pope.

AM: So, you got to see the pope?

Sister Luisa Teresa: Yes, of course. Close-up.

AM: You greeted each other?

Sister Luisa Teresa: I didn't get to greet him. I was close as he passed by, but not close enough to stretch out my hand to shake his hand. It happened at both fields [St. John Paul II Field and Santa María la Antigua Field].

AM: What is your age?

Sister Luisa Teresa: I am forty-three years consecrated in religious life [She thought I was asking how long she had been a nun.]

AM: Is it okay if I get your age? How old are you?

[She tells me she is sixty-four but young at heart; that is why she can accompany the youths and the young adults "in this precious journey in the faith. Our concrete objective in Cuba is to be missionaries of hope for a community that is struggling. We help them feel the gift, the gift of faith and hope—because Jesus is the center of life, and He never abandons us."]

AM: I am Panamanian—I was born here in Panama.

Sister Luisa Teresa: ¿*Panameño?*

AM: Yes, I was born in Colón. But we moved to New York in the United States when I was five years old.

Sister Luisa Teresa: Ha.

AM: Yes, so almost my entire life I have lived in the United States. It was important for me to come here as a journalist and as a Panamanian.

Sister Luisa Teresa: Of course.

AM: And as a Catholic.

Sister Luisa Teresa: Yes, of course. Blessed God *(Bendito Dios)*. A wonderful experience.

AM: I arrived here in Panama early yesterday morning, at about 5 a.m. So, I was here all day yesterday and all day today. I leave late tonight, at 11:30 from Tocumen Airport—where the pope is now. And I arrive in New York early tomorrow morning at about 5:30. From there I go to work to write the article [I laugh]. Very busy. Thank you much for the interview.

Sister Luisa Teresa: May God bless you—you have that as your mission *(Que Dios lo bendiga—tiene eso como su misión)*.

[She allowed me to take several photos of her as she sat at the table.]

AM: Gracias.

[I returned to my table and began organizing my notes, and I continued watching the farewell ceremony, looking up at the TV monitor on the wall. When I left later to take a taxi to the airport, the pope's plane had departed, and post-ceremony coverage continued. I believe the nun was still at her table when I left. I cannot remember for sure; everything was still kind of surreal.]

Pilgrims on the field awaiting the closing Mass Sunday morning.

Attentive pilgrims during the closing Mass.

Pilgrims leaving St. John Paul II Field after the Sunday morning closing Mass.

The McDonald's on Vía España, where the author interviewed Sister Luisa Teresa.

Pope Francis with bishops during the farewell ceremony Sunday evening at Tocumen International Airport. Machado captured this screen shot inside the McDonald's: TV coverage of the ceremony.

The plane on the Tocumen runway as it departs with the pope, en route to Rome (screen shot).

The pope's plane taking off from Tocumen on its way to Rome (screen shot).

Panama City skyline, photographed by the author from a shuttle bus for members of the press covering WYD Panama, after the Sunday morning closing Mass, en route from St. John Paul II Field back to the International Press Center (Atlapa Convention Center).

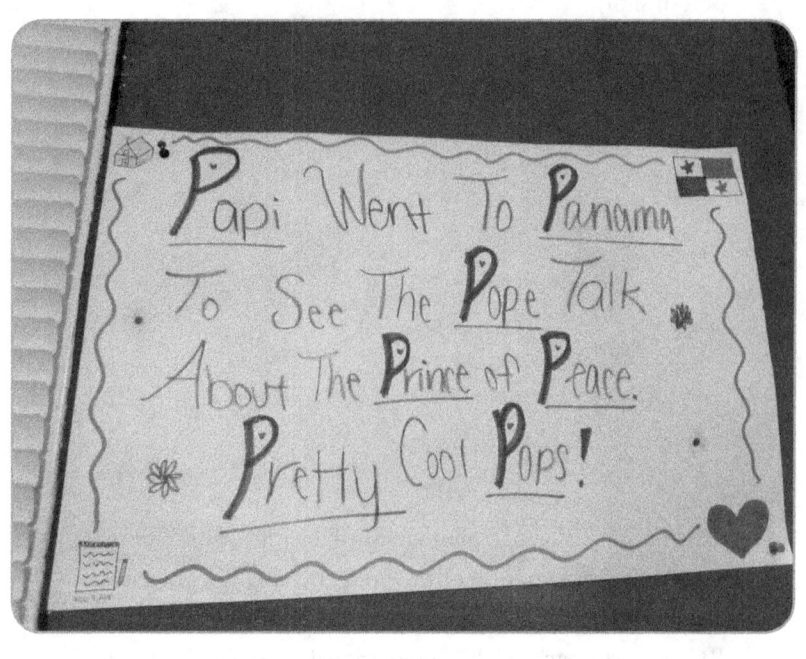

A poster made for Machado by the three youngest of his four daughters, about two weeks after World Youth Day Panama 2019 (His only son and first-born daughter are college grads, having long flown the nest).

TOCUMEN INTERNATIONAL AIRPORT

TOCUMEN INTERNATIONAL AIRPORT, SUNDAY NIGHT, JAN. 27:

Pierre Santos, 22, and a young woman named Ayse Divrikli, 20, from the Archdiocese of Malines, Brussels, in Belgium:

AM: WERE YOU here for the whole week, your group?
Pierre: Yes, the whole week, and before also.
AM: Before also? How come?
Ayes: Yes, we have been here for two weeks.
AM: Because? You were volunteering?
Ayes: No, no, because in Belgium we leave one week before to know a little bit more of the culture of Panama.
AM: Oh, to learn the culture.
Ayse: Yes.
Pierre: Yes.
AM: To do like tourists, sightseeing?
Pierre: Yes, but much more like education.
AM: Oh, educational and recreational?
Pierre: Yes.

AM: So, what day did you come?

Ayse: Jan. 12.

AM: So, from Jan. 12 to Jan. 27?

[Both say yes.]

AM: Was the group at the Mass this morning?

Pierre: Yes.

AM: Were you close, or far away, or in the middle?

Pierre: In between.

AM: What was your section?

Pierre: B-3. So not so far and not too much close, like in the middle.

AM: Oh, I see. And can you tell me what you thought about this morning, a lot of people.

And this whole week, what did it do for you spiritually?

Pierre: Spiritually, we do some prayer [this week] with the chief of the priests. I don't know how to say in English.

AM: Bishop.

Pierre: Yes. We exchanged our experience with the others in the groups, and we speak about to know each other.

Ayse: I think it's a pretty message [pope asserting that youths are the now of the Church, the present.] We talked with the group after the [closing] Mass, and we were all touched by what the pope said.

AM: Were you at the prayer vigil last night? Did you stay overnight?

[Both say yes].

Pierre: All my life I have been Catholic. My origins are Portuguese. So in Portugal there are a lot of Catholics. [He was born in Belgium of Portuguese ancestry.] My mom always learn me some prayers—they [his parents] follow the line of the Catholic spirit.

Ayse: I was born in Belgium, but I was raised in Polish ways. [Both her parents are from Poland.]

AM: So both your parents are from Poland, like John Paul II?

[Ayes says yes with a smile.]

AM: Do you need to go? Just one more thing.

Pierre: Sorry, we have to go (He says this after a woman calls for him and Ayse].

AM Oh, you have to go? Okay, thank you.

[Both say good-bye, smiling, as they join their group going into the luggage check-in area.]

Father Ferdinand Mushagalusa, 57, of the Congo, with the Father Barnabite Congregation:

(Father Ferdinand is a coordinator with Ayse and Peirre's group; he walked toward me as Ayse and Pierre headed to luggage check-in)

Father Ferdinand: *Hola.*

AM: *Hola.* Are you with—did you go to World Youth Day?

Father Ferdinand: I'm priest in Belgium.

AM: Oh, you are with that group? [I gesture toward Ayse and Pierre's group.]

Father Ferdinand: Yes.

AM: Oh, good to meet you. My name is Armando, with Catholic New York [I give him my business card.]

Father Ferdinand looks at the card and says: Armando Makadu.

AM: Machado.

Father Ferdinand: From here?

AM: Yeah. No, no, from New York—New York.

Father Ferdinand: New York, hah.

AM: Archdiocese of New York. I am going back to New York. But I was born here in Panama, in Colón, Panamá.

Father Ferdinand: You were born here?

AM: Yes, but when I was a little kid, five years old, we moved to New York.

Father Ferdinand: I'm Congolese, from Africa, but I'm priest missionary in Belgium.

AM: In the Archdiocese of Malines-Brussels?

Father Ferdinand: In the Diocese of Tournai [also in Belgium].

AM: Oh, I see. So could I get a few words from you too for the article?

Father Ferdinand: In English, in French or in Italian?

AM: In English. What is your first name?

Father Ferdinand: Father Ferdinand.

[I write it correctly in my notebook, show it to him and ask, "Like that, right?" And he says, *sí*.

AM: And what is your last name? [He spells it for me, some letters uttered in Spanish, and I write it down and show it to him and he says it is correct.]

Father Ferdinand: Yes, Mushagalusa.

AM: How do you pronounce it?

Father Ferdinand: Mushagalusa.

AM: Can you tell me your impression of the whole week and everything with the father—huh the huh pope? [I am speaking hurriedly, eager to get good comments from him and cognizant that he too will soon tell me he has to join the Belgium group at the luggage check-in area.]

Father Ferdinand: I can't speak well English, but this moment with the pope, is one moment *muy* important because the pope gave us lessons for all the priests and sisters to do, to have.

AM: Oh, I see. Oh, Okay.

Father Ferdinand: All persons must get Jesus in center of his life. When Jesus is to center of our life, all things must be well.

AM: How long have you been a priest, how many years?

Father Ferdinand: Five years, with the Father Barnabite Congregation.

AM: So you're originally from what country in Africa?

Father Ferdinand: The Democratic Republic of Congo, but a missionary in Belgium.

AM: Okay, Father, thank you much.

Father Ferdinand: Thank you, Armando.

[He starts walking toward Pierre, Ayse and the rest of the Belgium group.]

Joo Hyun Lee, 28, WYD volunteer, from the Archdiocese of Seoul, South Korea:

AM: Can you give me your age? How old are you?

Joo: Twenty-eight.

AM: Oh, you are a young adult, too.

[He laughs, and so do I.]

Joo: Thank you so much.

[He said in all there were an estimated four-hundred pilgrims and coordinators from South Korea, from several dioceses and ministries.]

Joo: I was here for two weeks.

[He arrived early to help with preparation work.]

AM: ¿Habla español?

Joo: Oh, no, no. I know French [He laughs]. I felt such a warm welcoming in Panama. It's very, very good message for me and for my friends, because I think God is around me every day. [He liked the pope's message about youth being the now, the present, of the Church.] I listened to the homily of Pope Francis, after then I think: God is living in me, in my mind and my heart, in my spirit. So, I accept. I pray. Everywhere, every time. I listen to the charisma of Pope Francis.

But before I studied for master course in university, I work in...South Korea [He was telling me what type of work he did before studying toward a master's degree; but I could not understand him, nor could I decipher it on my recording.] I think in society, it is difficult for living in society for Christians. Because every time I face choice for Christian or for society member, Catholic Church has helped me about choice very well.

[Despite his difficulty with English, Joo was clearly intimating that the faith has helped him to make the right choices in his life.]

AM: You mean making good choices, doing the right thing?
Joo: Yeah, yeah, good choices.
AM: Oh, I see, since you were a little kid.
Joo: Yeah, yeah. You from New York?
AM: Yes, New York.
Joo: My friend study in Brooklyn.
AM: Oh, yeah, the Brooklyn Diocese?
Joo: Yeah, Brooklyn Diocese.
AM: They are close together—Diocese of Brooklyn and Archdiocese of New York.
Joo: Three months ago, I went to New York.
AM: Oh, really?
Joo: Yes, I was in New York.
AM: So it's Joo Hyun Lee. [I show him my notebook, pointing to where he wrote his name for me.]

Joo: Yes.
AM: *Muchas gracias.*
Joo: *Muchas gracias—de nada.*
AM: *Merci.*
Joo: *Merci beaucoup* [We both laugh.]
AM: Thank you very much. Have a good trip.
[We walk away in different directions within Tocumen airport.]

A SHORT WHILE LATER, ALSO INSIDE THE AIRPORT TERMINAL:

Bernadette Salda and her sister Christina Salda, from the Diocese of Meaux, France, translated from Spanish:

(They are French. They speak some Spanish with a French accent, less English. Their group had forty-four pilgrims, five lay leaders, and two priests. I interviewed the Salda sisters while sitting on a bench in the airport, in Spanish and some English. They responded mostly in Spanish, but this is translated.)

Bernadette, 25:
AM: What is your name?
Bernadette: Bernadette, like the saint of Lourdes in France.
AM: Beautiful name *(oh, muy bonito, Bernadette)*. You were here for the whole week, *(una semana)*?
Bernadette: Two weeks in Panama.
AM: Oh, so you came a week before it began, before WYD?
Bernadette: Yes. *(Sí).*
AM: To see the country, to take tours?
Bernadette: Yes, in the town of Guararé, I got to know the people of Panama.

AM: Did you go to the closing Mass this morning?

Bernadette: Yes.

AM: Were you close or far from the stage, the altar?

Bernadette: Yes, close.

AM: Very close?

Bernadette: In Section 2.

AM: Where there were chairs? Where people were sitting on chairs?

Bernadette: No, no. [She gestured that her group was in an area with no chairs set up, just ground where pilgrims were sitting on their own lawn chairs or blankets, or standing; so the Salda sisters' group was close to the stage but not that close.]

AM: How did you like the pope's message, his homily message – *(¿Su homilía. cómo te gusto el mensaje del papa?)*

Bernadette: *¿Cómo me gusto?* (How did I like the homily?). For me, the words of the pope are very important, because he knows how to speak to the youths, to the young people. And it is a message of love, and of hope. It gives me energy to live with my Church.

AM: Oh, yes—to live with your Church?

Bernadette: Yes, very much.

AM: Can you tell me why the Catholic faith is important for you and your family? *(¿Por qué es importante?)*

Bernadette: Because in our lives, God does a lot. And because we see that without God in our lives, there is no—how do you say? There is no path. *(No hay camino)*. Yes, there is no good path. Because for us, God is like the light.

AM: The Light of Christ?

Bernadette: Yes. The Light of Christ that gives the path to live, to live good.

AM: Yes. The pope says we must maintain Christ at the center, at the center of our lives.

Bernadette: Yes, the center of life.

AM: Very important.

Bernadette: Yes.

AM: So, it isn't the Archdiocese of Paris?

Bernadette: No, *(cerca.)* It is near.

AM: What is the name?

Bernadette: Diocese of Meaux.

[Bernadette then introduced me to her sister Christina, who approached us from several feet away, where she had been conversing with other group members. I asked Christina if I could interview her as well. She said yes.]

Christina, 24:

AM: What did you think of the pope's message from this morning?

Christina: His message is one of much joy and hope for the youths. He gives a good message, a good message of peace. And a lesson—a lesson of peace for all the youths, and for all the adults. The pope touches everyone with this message.

AM: Why is the Catholic faith important to you?

Christina: Because we are all united for one person, one God. It is my faith; it is why I am filled with joy.

AM: Okay, Christina, thank you very much. *Muchas gracias.*

Christina: *Muchas gracias.*

AM: *Merci, merci.*

Christina: *Hah, bien!* Oh, good! [With a smile.]

AM: *Merci.* I know *un poquito—muy poquito* French. (I know a little French, very little).

[We both laugh—and I exchange Good-byes (*Adiós, Au revoir*) with her and Bernadette. Then members of their group stood up from nearby benches, and from the floor; they evidently had been waiting for Christina and Bernadette to finish talking with me. Conversing in French, the Salda sisters and their group began walking toward their gate to board their plane. I believe the two sisters said the group would be stopping in Miami to board another plane to France.]

AM Reflection:

It is now November 2019, ten months since WYD Panama, and the pope is under unusual attack, unprecedented ideological assaults on a papacy, from within the Church. I pray for him—*nuestro Papa Francisco*. I pray for him. And the faithful multitudes—they pray for him.

I have heard that young newlyweds are at the dawn of their marriage, and elderly couples are near the sunset of theirs (till death do them part). After World Youth Day Panama, it soon became clear to me that for the pilgrims I spoke with, this world-class retreat was the dawn of a new faith journey, their new spiritual trek.

Or it can be said that it was a turning point in their ongoing journey, a before and after division in time—before Panama and after Panama. It also became clear to me that this magnificent experience had a similar special significance for this journalist turned unofficial pilgrim.

The End *(Fin)*

AUTHOR'S NOTES

THREE SIDE NOTES:

- I have always admired the pope's call, indeed a longtime Church call, for Christian unity and interfaith dialogue.
- Words that have stayed with me: On Sunday Jan. 5, 2020, toward the end of noon Mass at St. James Church, Red Bank, N.J., Father Vicente told the faithful, "May the Lord bless you from the darkness into His Light."
- Since my college years, this Holy Bible verse has been a primary source of spiritual comfort for me, when Jesus said to his disciples: "These things I have spoken unto you, that in me ye might have peace. In the world ye shall have tribulation: but be of good cheer; I have overcome the world." (John 16:33).

ALSO OF NOTE:

I put my final writings for Two Days in Panama aside over most of the winter, just proofreading and editing now and then. It is now early May 2020, and an unprecedented health crisis called Covid-19 has the world, and mankind, overwhelmed with uncertainty, and for many, fear. Pope Francis, after his live-streamed Easter Sunday Mass (on April 12), told us in his Easter message *"urbi et orbi"* (to the city and the world):

"Like a new flame, this Good News springs up in the night; the night of a world already faced with epochal challenges and now oppressed by a pandemic severely testing our whole human family. In this night, the Church's voice rings out, 'Christ, my hope, is risen!'…The Risen Lord is also the Crucified One, not someone else. In his glorious body he bears indelible wounds; wounds that have become windows of hope.

Let us turn our gaze to him that he may heal the wounds of an afflicted humanity… May Christ, who has already defeated death and opened for us the way to eternal salvation, dispel the darkness of our suffering humanity and lead us into the light of his glorious day, a day that knows no end."

The pope was inside St. Peter's Basilica at the Vatican. He celebrated the Mass with no faithful in attendance because of the coronavirus pandemic.

ABOUT THE AUTHOR

Armando Machado is a longtime news writer and strong believer in trusting in the Lord. He has received several journalism awards. He was born in Colón, Panama, and raised in New York. He is a married father of five and holds a bachelor's degree in Liberal Arts from SUNY at Stony Brook, with minors in Journalism and English.

Machado lived in Western Washington for many years and returned to the Northeast in 2014, settling in Monmouth County, N.J., He enjoys playing basketball with his son and volleyball with his daughters, and taking family strolls on the boardwalk. The family has a cat and two parakeets.